B... Paradis
S.

MW01484981

B... Paradis
S.

The Lobster Theory
(and other analogies for jazz improvisation)

by Greg Fishman

GREG FISHMAN
JAZZ STUDIOS

Published by Greg Fishman Jazz Studios
Evanston, Illinois 60202

ISBN: 978-0-9914078-0-4

©2014 Greg Fishman. All rights reserved. International copyright secured.

No part of this book may be reproduced or transmitted in any form or by any means, electronic or mechanical, including photocopying or recording, or by any information storage and retrieval system, without permission in writing from the publisher. Violation of copyright is subject to all applicable laws.

Published by Greg Fishman Jazz Studios
824 Custer Avenue, Evanston, Illinois 60202
www.gregfishmanjazzstudios.com

The Lobster Theory

(and other analogies for jazz improvisation)

By Greg Fishman

TABLE OF CONTENTS

©2014 Greg Fishman
All rights reserved. International copyright secured.

Foreword

Wow! I have just finished reading through Greg Fishman's latest book *The Lobster Theory (and other analogies for jazz improvisation)*. He should be drawn and buttered for writing this! Seriously though, I am thrilled that this book is available!

I have known Greg for a number of years and I know some of his students. I have also checked out his other books…which are all fantastic and practical and are some of the very best on the market. I find his concepts and educational approach to be holistic and he tends to use analogies and imagery to great effect. I can appreciate this on many levels. I also love using analogies and visuals when I teach and I believe it helps students think outside the box and encourages them to be more creative and visual in their musical and improvisational approaches.

What Greg has accomplished in this book is to explain, and then show – through the use of awesome drawings and complete musical examples – different concepts and ideas that are essential to our development as musicians. From "Harmonic GPS" and "Ketchup on a Brownie" to "The Lobster Theory" and "Polishing the Silver" to "The Snake" and "Harmonic Turn Signals," "The School Bell" and "The Bus"…Greg covers particular musical concepts in very unusual but fulfilling and exciting ways. He provides personal stories that will initially draw in students and educators, then, he provides musical examples, cartoons, and sometimes an original tune that clearly exemplify and articulate the concepts and ideas he just explained!

We all have different learning styles and varying methods we use to understand concrete as well as esoteric concepts. I feel each of these chapters acknowledges the different ways that students learn and provides a truly holistic approach to teaching. They are aural, visual and tactile all at the same time.

Greg Fishman is a great educator who has the ability to recognize that it's essential to provide a variety of learning styles and patterns for the variety of ways we learn. *The Lobster Theory* is a really fun read and I enjoy Greg's sense of humor and wit. I truly feel the ideas he presents here are effective, long lasting and inviting for students and educators alike. I appreciate that Greg is curious, open, thoughtful, kind and honest with his students and with his approach to teaching. This is yet another in the long line of great music education books by Greg Fishman.

~ Jeff Coffin

Jeff Coffin is a three-time Grammy award winner and internationally recognized saxophonist, bandleader, composer and educator and has been traveling the globe since the late 20th Century. From 1997-2010, Coffin was a member of groundbreaking and genre-defying fusion group, Bela Fleck & the Flecktones. In mid 2008, Jeff also began touring with Dave Matthews Band after DMB founding saxophonist LeRoi Moore was injured, and officially joined the group in 2009 following his tragic passing. When not on the road with DMB, Coffin fronts his own group, Jeff Coffin & the Mu'tet and has presented over 300 music clinics as a Yamaha and D'Addario Performing Artist.

Preface

The Lobster Theory (and other analogies for jazz improvisation) is a new approach to learning the language of jazz. It's a book of musical concepts brought to life through the use of analogies, beautifully illustrated by *New Yorker* cartoonist Mick Stevens. The analogies teach complex musical ideas in a fun, friendly way, using everyday experiences from common situations.

Through these analogies I create a link between things you already know from other parts of your life, such as driving, eating, working out, etc., and show you how to use these experiences to help you achieve your goals in music.

Although music is an aural art form, not everyone has an aural learning style. All of us use our five senses (sight, sound, taste, smell and touch) to learn about the world around us.

Many people are visual learners, and they need to see an image in order to internalize a concept. Some are auditory learners, relying primarily on the sounds around them to process new information. Others are kinesthetic learners, responding to the way things feel, smell or taste.

With these different learning styles in mind, in order to make the analogies instantly relatable, I often use synesthesia, a mixing of the senses, to get my point across. For example, I might combine the sense of taste with sound, equating a flavor with a particular sound, describing a major seventh chord as a "sweet apple" and a diminished chord as a "tart apple." Or, I may use the image of a man fishing on a lake to convert the aural concept of accented notes into a visual perspective.

Many of the analogies are lighthearted and humorous, making them very user-friendly and easy to remember. The book is designed so that the chapters stand alone. You can read it cover-to-cover, or just go directly to any chapter that appeals to you.

Throughout the book, the imaginative illustrations by Mick Stevens convey the pure essence of my analogies. This unique combination of cartoons and analogies presents advanced musical concepts in an accessible way that everyone can enjoy.

~ Greg Fishman

Credits

Written by: Greg Fishman
Illustrations by: Mick Stevens
Foreword by: Jeff Coffin
Graphic Design and Book Layout by: Susanna Helman
Edited by: Jon Ziomek and Judy Roberts
Consultant: Doug Webb
Published by: Greg Fishman Jazz Studios, Evanston, Illinois

Greg Fishman is a D'Addario Woodwind artist and plays Rico reeds exclusively.

The Lobster Theory
(and other analogies for jazz improvisation)

4/21/16

Lifting Weights

It's January 1st, and your New Year's resolution is to get in shape and start working out every day. You've decided that you're going to do a one-hour workout each day at the gym, doing sets with a 100-pound weight. You're making good progress, and you're developing some muscle tone. This goes great for about a week.

ONE HOUR
OF
PRACTICE TIME
= 100 LBS.

PRACTICING ONE HOUR EVERY DAY

One day during the second week, you get busy with other things, and you miss a day at the gym. So you go in the next day, but even though the weight may *look* the same, it now feels like it weighs 200 pounds. You struggle with it, and you make it through the workout, but your form is getting sloppy, and you're straining.

The third week, you're just not in the mood for your workout. You miss seven days! You start feeling guilty (and you see your muscle tone disappearing), so you finally go back to the gym, ready to begin again, but now the weight feels like 700 pounds. That's the 100 pounds you were supposed to lift each day, times the seven days you missed.

CATCHING UP ON SEVEN DAYS OF
NOT PRACTICING

It's the same with music. As long as you practice every day, you'll improve, and you'll even build up to heavier "weights," represented by more challenging musical material.

However, if you miss a day and try to make up for it by practicing twice as long the next day, it's not as effective. In theory, it may seem that two hours of practice on Tuesday will give you the same results as one hour of practice on Monday and one hour of practice on Tuesday, but that's wrong. Something extraordinary happens when you practice and then put down your instrument to go on with the rest of your day. Your brain subconsciously digests the material you practiced, preparing you to reach deeper levels of understanding of the material for your next practice session.

Some of this processing is a memory of the physical moves you make on your instrument (muscle memory), and some of it is the absorption of the musical information (ear-training, rhythm, melodic and harmonic memory). If you miss a day, there's really no way to make up for that lost processing time.

Practicing every day is a great way to make a commitment to something that's important to you, and to get a better sense of order in your life. It's almost like setting aside time for meditation. Personally, I look at practicing as my own way of meditating. It clears my mind and improves my focus.

Certainly, there will be times in your life when it is simply impossible to practice each day. It's not going to be the end of your musical world if you miss a day or two of practice every once in a while, but you'll play better, feel better, and get much more enjoyment from music if you make a commitment to yourself to practice each and every day.

I always tell students that if they're really short on time, rather than missing practice completely, just ten minutes a day will make a big difference in their progress. This will give the brain something to process when you put your instrument down. Happy practicing!

The School Bell

Developing the ability to hear a sound and immediately locate that sound on your instrument is an essential part of establishing a strong connection between what you hear and what you play.

When I was in high school, one of our band rehearsals ran a bit late, and the class bell rang while I still had my saxophone out. Just for fun, I imitated the sound of the school bell with my horn and figured out that it was my F#. From that day forward, every time I heard that bell, I would play "air saxophone," doing the fingerings for my F#. It turned into a fun game for me.

After a while, I didn't even need to hear the bell. I could just put my fingers into the position of the F# fingering (without needing the horn), and I could sing the right note!

After a short time, I started using the everyday sounds around me to train my ear and my fingers to locate various notes on my horn. See how many everyday sounds you can use to strengthen your connection to your instrument, including…

The Alarm Clock

The Cell Phone

Now that you're aware of these sounds around you, utilize them to give yourself an ear training boost throughout the day. It's really an ear-opener when you start to notice that virtually any sound around you can be a note…a squeaky door hinge, the "ding" of an elevator arriving at your floor, the beep of a microwave timer…the list goes on and on.

This whole approach is part of an overall view I hold that I'm a musician 24/7, not just when I have my saxophone in my hands. It makes the time away from my horn more fun, and it keeps my mind and ears engaged. So, the next time you hear the whistle of your teakettle, go ahead and figure out the note it's been playing for you all these years!

The Car Horn

Ketchup on a Brownie

I was at a restaurant having lunch with some friends, and we were served brownies for dessert. As a joke, one of them grabbed a bottle of ketchup and pretended that he was pouring it on the brownies. I immediately got the sensation of an E natural over a C minor chord and said, "That's it! That's what I've been looking for!" That situation gave me the idea for the "Ketchup on a Brownie" analogy.

Try mentioning ketchup on a brownie to most people, and you'll almost always get an immediate, "Yuck"! That instant response is similar to the feeling that a good musician gets in his gut when he hears a note that clashes with a chord.

One day, a student wanted me to listen to a recording he'd made for a school audition. As I listened, I could hear that some of his notes were clashing with the chords. I mentioned this after we listened, and he told me that he didn't hear anything wrong. I could see that he felt bad about my comments, but I wasn't trying to hurt his feelings. I wanted to help him learn to hear what I was hearing.

We listened again, and this time, at the first clash, I stopped the recording at a spot where he was playing a major third (an E) against a C minor chord (which has an Eb for the third). I asked him to sing the note from his solo out loud. While he sang the note, I played the chord on the piano. He immediately heard the clash and adjusted the note to an Eb so that it fit the chord. The fact that he heard the clash and adjusted the note told me that he had good musical instincts.

I asked him to sing the note again, but not to adjust it. I wanted him to really get a good taste of what it was like to hear that E over the

C minor chord. So, he held out the note and I played the chord. We both started laughing. It was so awful-sounding that it was funny! I told him, "Now you know what ketchup on a brownie *sounds* like!"

In case you're interested in more examples of "ketchup-on-a-brownie" types of clashes, try these: B natural over a C7 chord (C-E-G-Bb) and a G natural over a Cmi7b5 chord (C-Eb-Gb-Bb). These sound truly awful!

This situation of unintentional clashing or "wrong" notes is quite common. Aspiring players often get distracted while soloing, thinking about what scale they're supposed to be playing, when they really should be *listening* to the way that each of their notes sounds over the chords.

Another reason for the "Ketchup on a Brownie" effect is the simple fact that some students have not actually taken the time to properly learn their chords. Learning the chords isn't just about playing them as part of a practice routine to improve your technique. It's also about internalizing the sounds of the chord structures so that you can hear if a note you're playing either fits, or is clashing.

Sometimes a clashing note can actually be a good thing. Often, professional players will intentionally play notes with a precisely controlled, well-calculated, built-in clash to produce a special effect or mood. By contrast, amateur players will play lots of unintentional clashing notes because they're lost in the song or don't know their scales and chords. The amateur's notes come across as mistakes, because they're played at random and without intent.

In this drawing, the customer is shocked by what the waiter is doing. The waiter *thinks* that he's pouring chocolate syrup on the brownie, but he grabbed the ketchup bottle by mistake, and never noticed. He's not even looking at the brownie, or at the face of the customer, for that matter.

This waiter isn't a bad guy. He just doesn't have a clue that he's doing anything wrong. The same is true of the amateur player. He means well. He's not *trying* to pour ketchup on the song, but the fact is that he's doing it, just like the waiter.

The customer in this drawing is like your listener. Please pay close attention to your notes, and don't pour ketchup on his brownies!

Polishing the Silver

As I was practicing chord arpeggios, I began thinking about how many years I've been playing, and how many decades I've been starting my practice sessions with a review of my chords. Why do I keep reviewing the same chords, year after year? As I continued to practice, I developed an interesting answer to my question. It was like polishing the silver for a dinner party.

Imagine that all chord structures are like pieces of fine silver cutlery. When polished, the silver is beautiful and gleaming, but when it's not polished, it's tarnished and dull.

Next, imagine that you've got close friends coming to your house for a dinner party, and you're about to set the table when you see that you forgot to polish the silver. You open the drawer, and it's a big mess of tarnished forks, spoons and knives. You start polishing furiously, and finish just a couple of pieces when the doorbell rings.

When you're improvising on a song, each new chord change represents another friend ringing your doorbell, looking forward to dinner.

Above: The amateur player's drawer of silverware.

You want to make sure that each new guest has clean, gleaming cutlery next to his dinner plate.

Because you have so many great friends, you just never know who's going to show up for dinner. Maybe a three-chord blues shows up at your door. That's like three people showing up for dinner. You always have a couple of place settings polished and looking nice. No problem. However, what if your old friend "Rhythm Changes" stops by for a surprise visit? There are usually 50 chords (some of them repeat) in those 32 measures. That's a lot of silver! What will you do if you only have two or three chords polished and ready to go? It's embarrassing to be caught unprepared for your guests.

This is why it's necessary to constantly polish your silverware, so it's shiny and clean, and ready for serving – even if "Cherokee" and "Giant Steps" were to show up at your door, ready to join you for dinner.

Polishing silver takes a long time and a lot of care. The longer you wait to polish it, the longer it takes to get the job done. However, if you keep the silver polished and ready to go, everything will always be ready for dinner in a "Moment's Notice."

Above: The professional player's drawer of silverware.

The Bus

I was coaching a combo at a jazz workshop when this analogy came to me.

Most of the players in the group were in their teens, except for the pianist, an older man who was constantly getting upset with himself. Every time he'd make a mistake, he'd swear and pound on the piano. He was disruptive, and he was scaring the young people. Everyone would look at me with uncomfortable stares when this guy would go into his latest harangue about the wrong notes in his solos.

I noticed that the guy was always getting lost in the chord progression. He seemed to know his chords, but during his solos, he was often in the wrong measure of the song because he'd start his phrases in a random fashion. In the middle of one of his rants, I interrupted him and asked:

"Have you ever taken a bus to get somewhere"?

The question seemed to startle him, and he looked at me, a little annoyed, and he said:

"Of course, I've taken a bus. What does that have to do with anything"?

I replied, "What happens if you get on the wrong bus"?

He was still upset, and looking down at the floor as he responded:

"You feel like a fool when you get on the wrong bus. You don't know where you're going."

Then, this analogy came into my mind, and I said, "Imagine that the four beats in a measure of 4/4 time are like buses. There are four downbeats and four upbeats in the measure, so there are eight different buses."

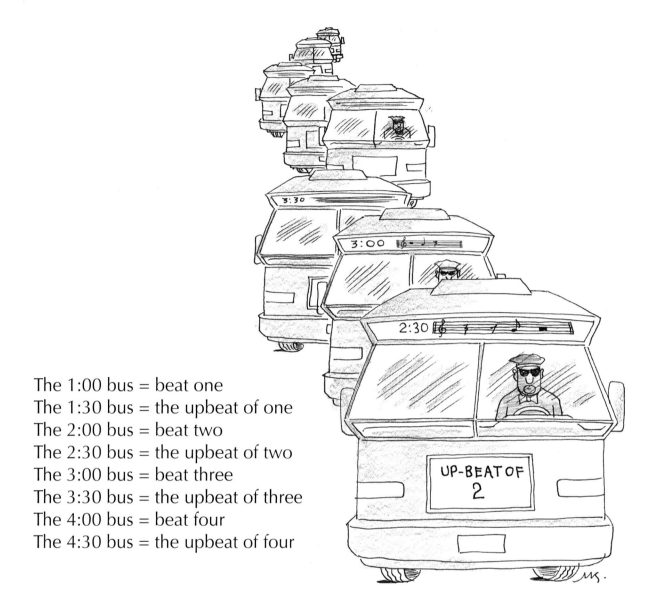

The 1:00 bus = beat one
The 1:30 bus = the upbeat of one
The 2:00 bus = beat two
The 2:30 bus = the upbeat of two
The 3:00 bus = beat three
The 3:30 bus = the upbeat of three
The 4:00 bus = beat four
The 4:30 bus = the upbeat of four

In order to be in control of your phrases, you need to get on the right bus. Let's say that you decide you're taking the 2:00 bus. This means that you need to start your improvised phrase on the second beat of the measure.

All buses take you *somewhere*, but in real life, you don't just wait for any bus. You wait for a *specific* bus. While you're waiting, lots of buses may pass by – but you're interested in only one bus. You want the one that takes you where you want to go.

So, the player needs to learn not to just take the first bus that comes along, but to make sure it's the right bus.

In other words, if you were waiting for the 1:30 bus, but got on the 3:00 bus by mistake, how long would it take you to realize that you're on the wrong bus? Would you ride it to the end of the line before realizing something was wrong, or would you get off the bus as soon as you discovered your mistake?

The beauty of the buses in music (as opposed to real life) is that they're always right on time. They're never late! If you miss the first 2:00 bus that comes by, no problem...just take the next one. Or, maybe the bus was too crowded because the piano player or drummer was playing a fill. Once again, you can simply wait for the next bus so that you don't bump into their musical fills when getting on the bus.

This phrase, starting on beat two, represents getting on the 2:00 bus.

The combo spent the next hour with everyone taking a turn riding the bus. To gain control of the different starting points in the measure, I would choose the bus in advance. For example, I'd say, "Three o'clock bus," and everyone would play a solo in which each improvised phrase would start on beat three. Phrases could be long or short. The only rule was that the players had to start on beat three.

As we started playing like this, the energy level of the group shot way up. This was a lot of fun! Instead of randomly running their scales, people were now strategizing how they'd initiate each phrase of their solos.

The bus analogy also had another great effect on the group. It dramatically increased everyone's concentration level, because now, each person in the group – even our previously cranky pianist – was actively listening to the soloist to determine if he was on the right or wrong bus. Just minutes before I told them about the buses, they were all just standing there, waiting for their own solos to start. They were ignoring each other, stuck in their own heads, thinking about what scale or lick they'd play when it was their turn to solo. Now, they were all actively *listening* and *learning* from each other with each phrase they played.

After everyone got comfortable riding just one bus for their solos, we started experimenting. I'd say, "Four o'clock bus (beat 4) followed by the two-thirty bus (the upbeat of 2)" and everyone would play their solos following those starting points for their phrases. After awhile, people in the group would shout out tricky combinations of buses, and we'd all try to play our solos with those starting points in mind.

At the very end of the session, I demonstrated a solo for the students in which I rode each of the eight buses, in order. That can be your own final test to show that you know how to take the right bus.

Play through the music examples on page 27, noticing the different effect the various "buses" have on the phrase. To help you focus on the unique feeling achieved by the various starting points, I've used the same basic phrase throughout the examples. The phrases starting on the downbeats have no pickup note, while the phrases starting on the upbeats have one pickup note. Once you get comfortable with this concept, feel free to improvise each phrase while keeping close track of your starting points.

The examples at letter A represent the downbeats of 1, 2, 3 and 4 as the 1:00, 2:00, 3:00 and 4:00 buses. The examples at letter B represent the upbeats of 1, 2, 3 and 4 as the 1:30, 2:30, 3:30 and 4:30 buses. (Notice that the 4:30 bus example has a triplet in the final beat of the second measure. This was necessary to fit the entire phrase into the allotted two measures.)

Letter C demonstrates the 3:30, 4:00 and 4:30 buses as pickups to the Dmi7 measure, as opposed to starting late in that measure. This approach can add excitement to the phrase, because it feels like you're anticipating the G7 chord ahead of time.

As a fun listening project, keep track of the buses used by your favorite soloists. You'll be amazed how much you can learn about their phrasing by learning their bus routes.

The bus analogy can also be used to control the end of your phrases. Once you've mastered the eight starting points, use this same concept to improve your control of the beat on which you end your phrases. For example, you can decide to end each phrase on the upbeat of two. This would be like stepping off of the 2:30 bus.

Controlling the end of each improvised phrase is more challenging than controlling the starting points. This is because you must keep track of your location within the measure while simultaneously creating your improvised phrase.

At the beginning of a new phrase (getting on the bus), you can easily count rests while choosing your staring point in the measure. Conversely, the ending of a phrase (getting off the bus) must be calculated while you're playing. Imagine that the final note of your phrase is the point at which you exit the bus.

Mastering the art of riding the buses will give your solos a sure-footed, appealing lift that will energize both the rhythm section and your audience.

THE BUS

GREG FISHMAN

SWING (♩ = 168)

1:00 Bus

2:00 Bus

3:00 Bus

4:00 Bus

1:30 Bus

2:30 Bus

3:30 Bus

4:30 Bus

3:30 Bus (as a pickup)

4:00 Bus (as a pickup)

4:30 Bus (as a pickup)

©2014 Greg Fishman Jazz Studios
All Rights Reserved. Copyright Secured.

Dual Citizen Notes

I was riding in the backseat of a taxi on my way home from the airport as I listened to the taxi driver tell me that in his old country, he was a doctor – but here in the U.S., he's a cab driver.

From the back seat, I could see his I.D. with his picture and his taxi number next to the meter on the passenger side of the dashboard. As he spoke, I imagined the look of the I.D. changing to fit his other profession as he told me about his previous job.

Shortly after that ride home in the taxi, I was teaching a music lesson, explaining to the student that a note could sound completely different if a new chord was played when that same note was repeated. At this point in the lesson, I was reminded of the taxi driver and his different jobs in different countries. His story was the inspiration for the analogy I now call "Dual Citizen Notes."

Dual Citizen Notes are common tones between chords. For example, if you think of the note "C," the first chord that usually comes to mind is a Cmaj7 chord. Some people would notice that the "C" is also the third of an Ami7 chord, the fifth of an F7 chord, the seventh of a Dmi7b5 chord, etc.

As an improvising musician, I've always felt that it was a fun part of my job to be able to identify the "countries" and "professions" of a note by hearing the way that the note sounds in different locations within a chord.

In each case, the note itself is the same, but its position changes in different chords – just as a person could have different jobs in different countries.

Let's anthropomorphize the note and call it "Mr. C." Also, let's refer to the chords as "countries." So, in the "country" of Cmaj7, the job of Mr. C is being the root. In the country of Ami7, his job is being the third, while in the country of F7, he's the fifth. In the land of DbMaj7, he's the seventh.

MUSICAL PASSPORT

COUNTRY	PROFESSION
C Maj7	Root
A mi7	b3rd
Ab Maj7	3rd
G7 sus 4	4th
F# dim7	b5th
F Maj7	5th
E 7#5 (Enharmonic for B#)	#5th
Ebmi6	6th
D7	7th
Db Maj7	Maj7th
B7b9	b9th
Bb mi9	9th
A7#9 (Enharmonic for B#)	#9th
G mi7	11th
Gb Maj7#11	#11th
E mi7b5	b13th
Eb13	13th

(And Many, Many More...)

If Mr. C is the root, maybe he's a bricklayer, laying down the foundation of the chord. If he's the third, maybe he's a fireman. If he's the fifth, maybe he's a teacher. If he's the seventh, perhaps he's a doctor.

The thing that's interesting is that all of the "jobs" are important. The root is a very important note, as is the third, the fifth, etc. Together, "chord countries" and their citizens, like Mr. C, work together to make up a beautiful and diverse harmonic world.

To get acquainted with the Dual Citizen Note concept, practice the chords listed in the passport drawing above, paying close attention to the sound of the C in each chord. There are lots of additional chords that also include "Mr. C." As a fun exercise, see how many you can find.

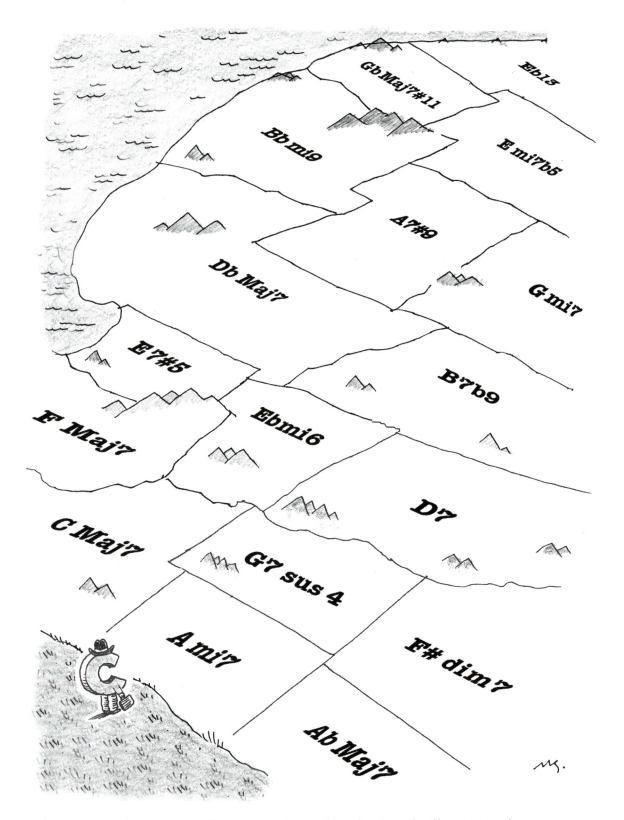
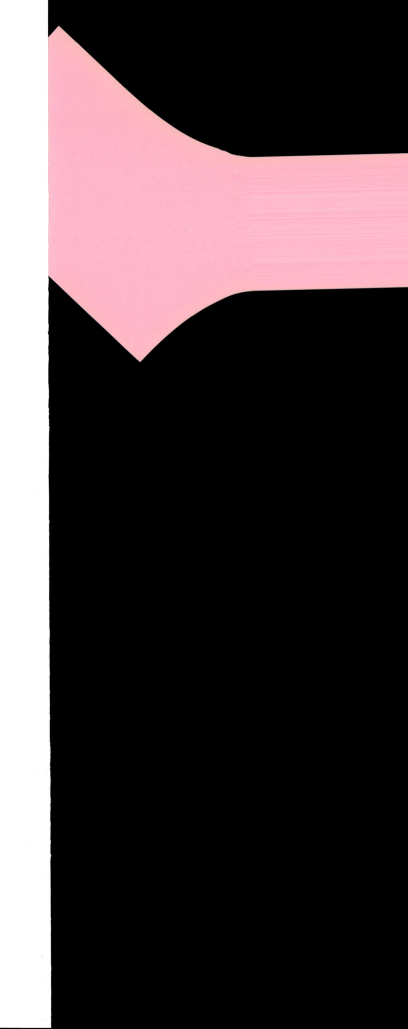

Above, Mr. C looks out at the wide variety of professions he'll enjoy in the many different chord countries.

The Lobster Theory

Did you ever wonder why good restaurants have live lobsters in a tank? Why don't they just have a bunch of lobsters in the refrigerator, next to the ribs and chicken? There's a good reason. It's because lobsters spoil immediately. In order to be fresh, the live lobster needs to go straight into the boiling pot of water. (My apologies to vegetarians reading this.)

Jazz is the same way – the ideas used for your improvised solos have a short shelf life. The ideas are like the lobsters. A new chord change represents the boiling pot of water. The idea you're about to play on that chord represents the lobster. The idea has to occur to you within a close proximity of the new chord so that it's fresh.

Let's say that your combo is about to play "Cherokee." If you're thinking ahead to the brilliant licks you're going to play on the bridge of your solo, you'll have what I call "dead lobsters." By deciding on the licks so far ahead of time, you've taken them out of the tank too soon, and these licks will likely sound contrived or "worked out." The notes will still fit the chords, but because they're not spontaneous, they won't sound exciting or in the moment.

This may seem to suggest that you shouldn't practice licks or patterns, for fear of dead lobsters. However, it's the opposite. In fact, your jazz vocabulary is like a tank of live lobsters. Each musical idea is a lobster. You'll need to have your vocabulary under your fingers and ready to play cleanly the moment the idea occurs to you.

When soloing, take the very first idea that occurs naturally to you. That idea represents the first lobster you grab from the tank. Amateur players are always second-guessing themselves, starting an idea and then abandoning it before they develop it. The professional player chooses an idea and develops it. When he's ready for the next musical idea, he'll reach into the tank and grab another lobster. Some amateur players have just one lobster in their tank. They use it, and they're suddenly left with an empty tank of water. The professional player's lobster tank is constantly replenishing itself, because with experience, he has learned to mix, edit, combine and even transpose the ideas. This is a good thing, because it keeps your lobster tank full.

Have you ever heard a jazz recording where a player starts his solo with the last few notes of the previous player's solo? That's the lobster theory in action! There's no way that the new soloist could have known, in advance, what the previous soloist would play at the end of his final phrase.

Starting your solo with the final phrase of the previous soloist is lots of fun and always done in the heat of the moment. I call these ideas "Imported lobsters." Imported lobsters can be added to your solo any time, and from any source within earshot. The piano player's comping rhythms and voicings, as well as the drummer's rhythms and patterns, are great sources for imported lobster. For example, if the drummer plays a catchy rhythm on his snare drum and you pick up on it and work it into your solo, that's an imported lobster. Mixing a few imported lobsters in with your own "domestic lobsters" always provides musical interaction with the group, and gives your solos life and energy.

Whether you have a live or dead lobster doesn't depend on the musical idea itself. Any idea could be live or dead. What makes it a "live" idea is the point in time when you think of it.

For example, if a C7 chord is coming up in the song's chord progression, take your C7 lobster out of the tank anywhere from a few beats before it's needed, up to the first beat of the C7 measure itself – and you'll have a live lobster.

Let's relate the lobster theory to a social situation. Have you ever been with some friends when you spontaneously comment on something that happens, and everyone laughs? That spontaneous comment you made was a live lobster. You used your existing vocabulary to make a comment that related to the context of the situation.

A few days later, you're with those same people and you want to get that big laugh again. So, you repeat your comment from the other day, but this time, it's not funny. You thought about it all day long, waiting to unleash it on your friends. It's a dead lobster. However, the first time you used it, it was alive and fresh because it fit the moment perfectly.

(No Lobsters Were Harmed in the Making of This Picture)

Professional musicians (and comedians and actors) develop the ability to recycle the same lobsters over and over again. They learn to recreate the spontaneous feeling of the original moment by reliving it as if it's happening for the first time. You can hear musical examples of this in many classic recordings where a jazz master plays one of his trademark licks. Although he may have played the lick a thousand times before, the way he places it in each new solo keeps it fresh and brimming with life, because it is experienced in the moment.

At this point, you might be wondering, "Where do the lobsters come from, anyway?" Good question! The lobsters come from all the musicians you listen to. Imagine that you're on a lobster boat, listening to John Coltrane (on the Coltrane Sea). Your ears are like lobster nets in the water, and the musical ideas you hear in Coltrane's solos are the lobsters. As you listen to Coltrane, your ears are catching ideas that look and sound like Coltrane. Next, let's say you've sailed your boat to the Stan Getz River. As your ears again cast the listening nets, they will catch lobsters that look and sound like Getz. You need to sail your lobster boat around the musical world to collect lots of different types of lobsters.

In just a few years, those lobsters will crossbreed in your tank (your mind), and you'll have a completely new species of lobster, bearing your own name. Your lobsters will have a combination of your favorite traits from all of the lobsters you've caught.

In the beginning, you'll use many lobsters from the established players of both the past and present to help get your sea legs in the jazz language. I call those ideas OPLs (Other Player's Lobsters). That's a great way to start, but don't neglect your "inner lobster."

Your inner lobster is the source of your own ideas. Just as you have the listening nets out to catch the ideas of others, you should have them out for yourself as well. Personally, I developed my inner lobster through the process of writing original compositions and soloing, as well as writing jazz etudes. Over time, you should introduce more and more of your own lobsters into your tank, so that your solos truly reflect your unique personality.

Of course, the meal isn't complete with just lobster. You need your side dishes, too. Maybe some sweet potatoes, corn on the cob, asparagus, etc. You provide these side dishes in your solo by creating additional musical phrases that blend well with your main course of lobster. When you develop a musical idea, it enhances the flavor even more, like dipping your lobster into melted butter. I'm going to dinner now. Lobster, anyone?

Harmonic GPS

When I was a kid, my dad had an old-fashioned compass in his car. I used to look at it to see which direction we were traveling. It was pretty cool, but with today's advances in technology, most cars have a GPS system to tell the driver not only the direction, but also the name of the street, the town, the state, etc.

It's one thing to know you're heading north, but it's another to know that you're heading north on Michigan Avenue, just past East Huron Street in Chicago, Illinois. This difference in detailed information between the compass and the GPS is the same difference between the way that a beginning player and a professional player hear their notes.

A compass gives you no context in regard to your location. It just tells you that you're heading north. You could be heading north any place in the world. Let's imagine that your compass is a Harmonic Compass, and that a reading of "north" is the equivalent of playing a "D" on the saxophone. You know that you're playing a "D," but you're not yet aware of the harmonic context of your note. It could be any degree of many different chords. This is the time to turn on your Harmonic GPS.

Your car's GPS provides very specific information about your location. Let's revisit our "D" on the saxophone. With the Harmonic GPS, we would know if the "D" was going to be the 9th of a Cmi7 chord, because we'd be hearing the note in harmonic context. Just as the GPS uses multiple satellites to triangulate your car's location, your ear needs to hear multiple notes within the chord to determine the harmonic location of your note.

To make the most of your Harmonic GPS, you need to develop the ability to hear your melody note as it relates to the chord. Many aspiring players have never given this concept a thought, mistakenly thinking that only pianists (or guitarists) need concern themselves with the chords. In fact, nothing could be further from the truth.

Play a "D" on the piano with the index finger of your right hand. By itself, it's like the compass. You know you're playing a "D," but beyond that, you don't know whether it's the root, third, fifth, seventh, etc., of a chord. You also don't know whether the underlying chord is going to be major, dominant, minor, etc. Next, with your left hand, play, from the bottom-up: C-Eb-G-Bb on the piano. Play the "D" again with your right hand as you let the notes in the chord continue to sustain. This is like the GPS telling you that the location of your note is the ninth of a minor seventh chord. You can now hear that the "D" is a major ninth above the root. You may also hear that the "D" is a major seventh above the third of the chord, a perfect fifth above the fifth of the chord, and a major third above the seventh of the chord. There's no longer any doubt about the location of your note and its relationship to the rest of the chord.

We could even take the analogy one step further and refer to the root, third, fifth and seventh of the chord as POIs (points of interest) in relation to your current location, just as your GPS can tell you the location of the closest restaurant, movie theater or gas station.

It wasn't until several years after I'd started studying the saxophone that I realized the importance of hearing the chords in this way. In order to improve my Harmonic GPS hearing, I studied jazz piano and spent a lot of time training my ear to hear and recognize all of the many different types of chords.

I took the harmonic concepts I'd learned from the study of piano, and integrated that knowledge into my saxophone playing. In time, I was able to imagine the sound of the full chord for each note I'd play on the saxophone. I could play the same "D" repeatedly on the sax and imagine it sounding like the root, third, fifth, seventh, ninth, etc. As an ear-training exercise, I'd play the "D" in the upper register of the saxophone, and then arpeggiate various chords in the lower register of the instrument. These chord arpeggios represented the left hand of the pianist, while the high "D" represented the right hand of the pianist.

If I had only known about this concept from day one, I could have saved myself a lot of time and effort, and my playing level would have progressed much more quickly. This is why I tell my students, right from the beginning, that they need to "hear like a piano player."

Think how cool it would be to play a single note on your horn and hear the entire chord clearly in your mind. It gives you a lot of confidence as a soloist, because you're hearing in a very specific way. You're no longer just playing any random note from a scale, but playing a specific note in a chord.

The aspiring saxophonist in the drawing below is hearing with a Harmonic Compass. In other words, he's hearing a "D" and he's playing a "D," but that's all that he's hearing in his mind. He's just playing that individual note,

Harmonic Compass

Hearing "Out of Harmonic Context" with a Harmonic Compass

with no harmonic context. He doesn't know if the note is the root, third, fifth, seventh, etc. That's just like the compass. It's like he knows he's headed north, but that's about all he knows. Hearing in this way is limiting, because you don't know enough about the location of your note within the chord to make the kinds of musical decisions that will get you safely to your musical destination.

The experienced saxophonist pictured below is playing with a Harmonic GPS. He is playing the same note as the player with the Harmonic Compass, but he's hearing the sound of the full chord in his mind, with his "D" as the ninth of a Cmi7 chord.

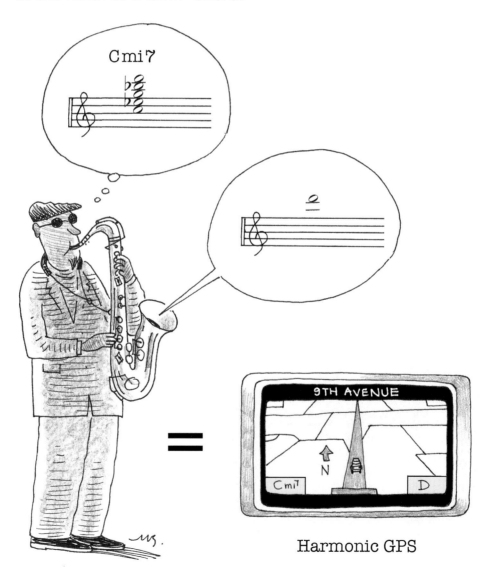

Hearing "In Harmonic Context" with a Harmonic GPS

Even though both saxophonists are playing the same note, the player using the Harmonic Compass will never achieve the same level of detail in the sound of his note as the player using the Harmonic GPS.

Another way to describe the difference between these two players would be to say that the player using the Harmonic Compass is hearing his note "out of harmonic context," while the player using the Harmonic GPS is hearing his note "in harmonic context."

Just in case it's still not clear to you why the Harmonic GPS approach is superior to the Harmonic Compass approach, let's look at this concept in terms of the word "stop." If you were asked to say the word "stop" out of context, you'd pronounce it properly and accurately, but without any emotion. Now, imagine that a reckless driver just went through a red light and nearly hit your car. You would shout, "Why didn't he *stop*?" The word "stop" is going to be uttered with very strong emotion. That's because the word is now being used in context, just like the pro is playing his note in context.

If you want your notes to communicate a strong feeling of emotion, you need to hear each of your notes in harmonic context. Whether you're playing with a pianist or playing unaccompanied, that extra feeling and depth will always be present in every note you play if you're hearing with a Harmonic GPS.

In the following excerpt from the etude "Cermak Road," I demonstrate the Harmonic GPS concept by combining three musical layers (melody, bass notes and chords) into a single horizontal line of notes.

Play through the examples on the next page while noticing the effect of adding the additional musical layers. Letter "A" features the original melody. Letter "B" adds the roots of the chords (bass notes) to the melody. Letter "C" combines the melody, bass notes and chord arpeggios. After you've played all three versions, play the original version at letter "A" once again while imagining the sound of the other two versions in your mind. This will give you a feeling of what it's like to hear a melody with a Harmonic GPS while playing a single-note instrument, such as a saxophone. It's like having the sound of a pianist in your mind, playing the perfect chords to compliment your chosen melody notes.

Excerpt of "Cermak Road," from
Jazz Saxophone Etudes - Vol. 3

Cermak Road

Greg Fishman

The original melody:

The original melody with roots of the chords added:

The original melody with full chords added:

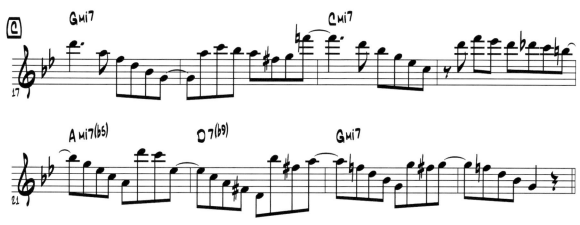

©2014 Greg Fishman Jazz Studios
All Rights Reserved. Copyright Secured.

If you can't improvise without a background track featuring a full rhythm section playing behind you, or without reading a lead-sheet with chord symbols, you probably don't yet have a fully functioning Harmonic GPS. No worries. The fact that you've just read this chapter means that you're now well on your way to trading in your old Harmonic Compass for a new, fully functional Harmonic GPS. It will take patience and practice when you first get your GPS up and running, but the musical benefits of hearing this way will stay with you for life.

The Waiter

You go to a nice restaurant and order a full dinner: soup, a main course, and a dessert. In a short time, the waiter brings your soup. It's a little too hot, but it's delicious. You're blowing on the spoon to cool it off, when the waiter comes and takes away the bowl of soup, replacing it with your main course, right under your dripping spoon.

This is what it's like for the listener if you don't take enough time to develop your ideas fully before moving on with your solo. It feels like the waiter is rushing you through your meal. You need the ability as a soloist to be patient enough to develop your musical ideas before you move on to new material in the solo.

This concept of knowing the right time to end one idea and start the next idea applies to all lengths of solos, whether they're eight measures or three choruses long.

Let's consider the same setup as above, but this time, something else strange happens. You take your time and finish your soup. It was delicious, but now you're ready for the main course. You wait with great anticipation. The waiter finally appears and takes away the empty soup bowl, but instead of serving your main course, he serves yet another bowl of soup!

This is what it's like for the listener if you don't know how to move past your opening idea into the solo's main course. It can feel like the same appetizer is being served over and over.

Once you have worked out the timing issues with the solo's appetizer, you can then move on to the main course. That's when the solo really starts to flow. Flavors blend and compliment each other as you take a bite of one idea, a sip of another idea, a taste of your musical side dish and then another bite of the main idea. It's a whirlwind of textures and flavors.

After the main course, it's time for dessert. The dessert should balance out your meal so that you've experienced just the right blend of flavors and textures. I've often heard aspiring players destroy what would otherwise have been a great musical meal by not knowing how to end their solo.

Just as an experienced waiter knows when his customer is ready for the next course, a good soloist knows when it's time to serve the next musical idea to the listener. The beginning, middle and end of a solo are like the appetizer, main course and dessert of a great meal. Dinner is served…

APPETIZER   MAIN   COURSE   DESSERT

Alligators, Elephants & Clowns

Memorizing the key signatures for the major scales has always been a challenge for music students. I can recall when I first learned my major scales. I memorized the key signatures by writing them out hundreds of times. I eventually learned to play the scales by sheer repetition, but it wasn't fun or easy.

Years later, when I first started teaching, I noticed my own students struggling, just as I had, with some of the "difficult" scales such as F# Major and Db Major. I realized that they were basically just guessing at the key signatures, instead of actually knowing them. I knew that there had to be a better system for learning the major scales than just playing them by rote, as I had done in my youth.

I started to experiment with different ways of teaching the scales. At first, I tried teaching them by intervals. You've probably seen this formula of whole-steps and half-steps to produce the sound of a major scale: WWHWWWH. While this system does produce the correct sounding sequence of notes, it does not actually teach students the key signatures. I knew that there had to be a better way.

About six months into my scale teaching experiments, I was writing out the number of flats and sharps in each scale for a student, when suddenly, a mathematical truth about the scales jumped out at me for the first time. I noticed that the number of flats plus the number of sharps for scales based on the same letter name always added up to the number seven!

For example:

F G A Bb C D E F = 1 flat
F# G# A# B C# D# E# F# = 6 sharps

_____

The combined number of flats + sharps = 7

I thought that it must be some kind of fluke. It just couldn't be that simple. As I went down the list of scales, I started laughing, because I saw that this system of adding up to the number seven worked for all of the scales. If only I'd known this when I first started playing, it would have been much easier for me to learn!

One really appealing element of this system is the fact that initially, it is only necessary to memorize the key signatures up to three flats and three sharps. You can then utilize the new system to figure out all of the remaining major scales. It's so easy that you'll be smiling as you read on!

Let's begin with the letters of the musical alphabet. The musical alphabet is made up of the letters A, B, C, D, E, F and G. All major scales consist of seven consecutive letters of the musical alphabet (plus an eighth letter repeating the first letter up an octave). The scales can start on any of the seven letter names.

With the exception of the letter C, each letter name of the musical alphabet has two major scales based on that same letter name (such as F and F#, or Bb and B), with one scale containing flats in the key signature, and the other scale containing sharps. The combined number of flats and sharps for all scales based on the same letter name always adds up to seven.

For example, the key of F Major has one flat. This means that the F# Major scale must have six sharps, because both scales are based on the same letter name (F), and 1 + 6 = 7.

Let's try a few more, just to get the hang of it. The Bb Major scale has two flats, which means that the B Major scale must have five sharps, because 2 + 5 = 7.

If someone were to ask you what scale has five flats, think about the scale that has two sharps. The key of D Major has two sharps, so the scale with five flats must be Db Major, because 2 + 5 = 7.

The letter name of C has three major scales: C, Cb and C#. The key of C Major has zero flats or sharps. The key of Cb Major has seven flats, and the key of C# Major has seven sharps. Once again, the number of flats plus sharps adds up to seven, because 0 + 7 = 7.

Although usually referred to as "the twelve major scales," there are actually fifteen major scales if you count the enharmonically equivalent scales: B Major sounds like Cb Major, F# Major sounds like Gb Major, and C# Major sounds like Db Major.

The table below shows all of the combinations of flats and sharps in the key signatures that add up to a total of seven:

Scales with Flats	Scales with Sharps	Total Number of Sharps & Flats
C = 0 Flats	C# = 7 Sharps	= 7
F = 1 Flat	F# = 6 Sharps	= 7
Bb = 2 Flats	B = 5 Sharps	= 7
Eb = 3 Flats	E = 4 Sharps	= 7
Ab = 4 Flats	A = 3 Sharps	= 7
Db = 5 Flats	D = 2 Sharps	= 7
Gb = 6 Flats	G = 1 Sharp	= 7
Cb = 7 Flats	C = 0 Sharps	= 7

At this point, you're probably asking yourself, "What in the world could alligators, elephants and clowns possibly have to do with major scales?" Good question! One of the interesting challenges I face as a teacher is to make learning fun and exciting for students of all ages.

ALLIGATORS

One day, while explaining the concept of key signatures, my beginning student was having some trouble remembering that the term "key signature" referred to the number of sharps or flats in a scale. I traced my car key on a piece of paper so that he could remember the concept, linking the idea quite literally to a "key."

After looking at the tracing of the key, I noticed that it resembled an alligator, with the top part of the key looking like the head, and the "teeth" of the key looking like the alligator's jaw. I counted the teeth on the key. There were six of them. Then, I labeled the drawing as the F# Major Scale (which has six sharps), and the "alligator analogy" was born. From that day forward, I started drawing alligators to teach the scales, using the number of teeth in their jaws as a way of identifying the sharps and flats in the key signatures.

In the illustration on the next page, you can easily see all of the key signatures of the major scales represented by the number of teeth in the upper and lower jaws of the alligators. Study the drawing so that you can picture it in your mind.

Count the number of teeth in the upper and lower jaws of each alligator. In each case, the total number is seven. The letter name of the scale is circled next to the jaw containing the correct number of sharps or flats for the scale. The upper jaws of the alligators represent the number of sharps, and the lower jaws represent the number of flats in the key signature.

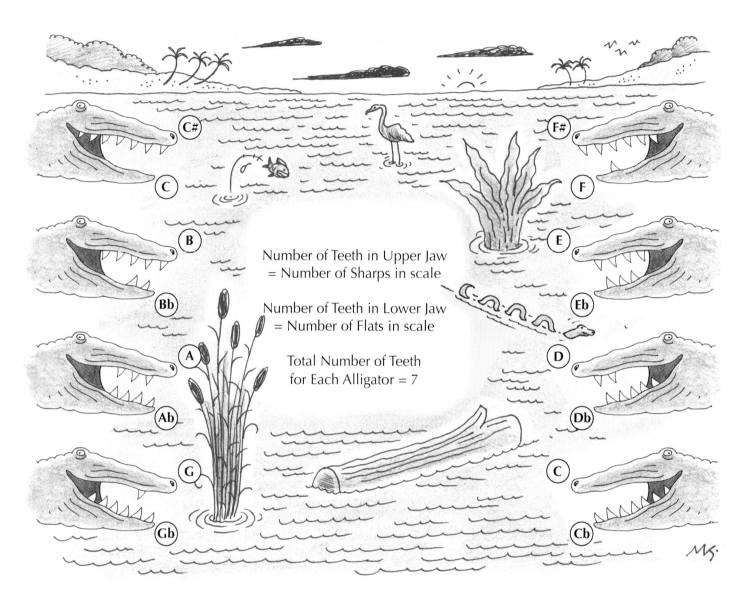

Number of Teeth in Upper Jaw
= Number of Sharps in scale

Number of Teeth in Lower Jaw
= Number of Flats in scale

Total Number of Teeth
for Each Alligator = 7

Alligators Have Seven Teeth

Now that we know how many flats or sharps are in each scale, we need to learn which notes are flatted or sharped. The flats and sharps occur in a specific order. I've created a couple of funny mnemonic sentences to help you easily remember the order of flats and sharps. A sentence about baby elephants will help you memorize the order of flats.

Baby Elephants Always Dig Good Clean Fun. (Order of flats)

BABY ELEPHANTS

Look at the picture above as you say this sentence out loud: "**B**aby **E**lephants **A**lways **D**ig **G**ood **C**lean **F**un." The first letter of each word in this sentence represents the flats in their proper order. Whenever you need to remember the order of flats, imagine this picture and say this sentence in your mind.

Let's start with the key of F Major. It has one flat. To figure out which note to flat, think of the first letter of the first word in the sentence. That word would be "**B**aby," so the flat in the key of F Major is Bb.

The key of Bb Major has two flats. What were the first two words of the sentence? "**B**aby **E**lephants." That means that the two flats in the key of Bb Major are Bb and Eb.

The key of Eb Major has three flats. Follow the same procedure as above. Think: "**B**aby **E**lephants **A**lways" and you'll know that the three flats in the key of Eb Major are Bb, Eb and Ab.

See the table below for all of the major scales with flats:

F Major (1 Flat)	Baby (Bb)
Bb Major (2 Flats)	Baby Elephants (Bb, Eb)
Eb Major (3 Flats)	Baby Elephants Always (Bb, Eb, Ab)
Ab Major (4 Flats)	Baby Elephants Always Dig (Bb, Eb, Ab, Db)
Db Major (5 Flats)	Baby Elephants Always Dig Good (Bb, Eb, Ab, Db, Gb)
Gb Major (6 Flats)	Baby Elephants Always Dig Good Clean (Bb, Eb, Ab, Db, Gb, Cb)
Cb Major (7 Flats)	Baby Elephants Always Dig Good Clean Fun (Bb, Eb, Ab, Db, Gb, Cb, Fb)

Next, let's learn the order of sharps. (The order of sharps is the reverse of the order of flats.) A sentence about funny clowns will help you memorize the order of sharps.

Funny Clowns Go Diving After Every Balloon. (Order of sharps)

FUNNY CLOWNS

Look at the picture above as you say the following sentence out loud: "**F**unny **C**lowns **G**o **D**iving **A**fter **E**very **B**alloon." The first letter of each word in this sentence represents the sharps in their proper order. Whenever you need to remember the order of sharps, imagine this picture and say this sentence in your mind, keeping track of the first letter of each word in the sentence.

Let's start with the key of G Major. It has one sharp. To figure out which note is sharped, simply recall the first letter of the first word in the sentence. That would be the word "**F**unny." The first letter in the word is "F." That means that the sharp in the key of G Major is F♯.

The key of D Major has two sharps. What were the first two words of the sentence? "**F**unny **C**lowns." That means that the two sharps in the key of D Major are F sharp and C sharp.

How about the key of A Major? It has three sharps. Which ones? Think of the first three words: "**F**unny **C**lowns **G**o."

See the table below for all of the major scales with sharps:

G Major (1 Sharp)	Funny (F#)
D Major (2 Sharps)	Funny Clowns (F#, C#)
A Major (3 Sharps)	Funny Clowns Go (F#, C#, G#)
E Major (4 Sharps)	Funny Clowns Go Diving (F#, C#, G#, D#)
B Major (5 Sharps)	Funny Clowns Go Diving After (F#, C#, G#, D#, A#)
F# Major (6 Sharps)	Funny Clowns Go Diving After Every (F#, C#, G#, D#, A#, E#)
C# Major (7 Sharps)	Funny Clowns Go Diving After Every Balloon (F#, C#, G#, D#, A#, E#, B#)

THINKING IN REVERSE

There's one additional scale system I'd like to share with you. I use it for students who relate more to mathematical concepts than to the drawings used above. I call this scale system "Thinking in Reverse." This will be especially useful when thinking of scales with high numbers of sharps or flats.

Let's look at the F Major scale. It has one flat (Bb). We know that the F# Major scale has six sharps, because 1 + 6 = 7, but here's something you might not have noticed: The note that was flat in the F scale (the Bb) is the same note that's natural in the F# scale (the B natural).

When I think of the F# Major scale with this system, I don't have to think about remembering six sharps. If I just think "in reverse," I can focus on the fact that the F# Major scale has one natural, B natural. Everything else is sharp by default. It's basically like an F Major scale, but with inverse accidentals. Look at the table below to help you visualize the "thinking in reverse" approach.

F#	G#	A#	B	C#	D#	E#	F#
F	G	A	Bb	C	D	E	F

Above: The F# Major and F Major Scales

Let's look at another example. The G scale has one sharp (F#). That means that the Gb scale has one natural (F natural) and all other notes are flat by default:

G	A	B	C	D	E	F#	G
Gb	Ab	Bb	Cb	Db	Eb	F	Gb

Above: The G Major and Gb Major Scales

By using the "thinking in reverse" concept, you can now look at the alligator drawing from another perspective. For example, if the alligator has two teeth in his upper jaw, you can now see those teeth acting not only as the two sharps in the key of D Major (F# and C#), but also as the only two naturals in the key of Db Major (F natural and C natural).

After you've memorized the key signatures for all of the major scales, take the time to practice them on your instrument. Remember to always play your scales with your best tone and with accurate time.

Also, be creative when practicing your scales. To really gain control of them you'll need to do more than just play them ascending and descending. Play them in intervals of 3rds, 4ths, 5ths, 6ths, 7ths, etc. Always use a wide variety of dynamics and articulations when practicing your scales.

Now that you know your key signatures, you're well on your way to becoming the best musician you can be. And, in case you happen to momentarily forget a key signature, just remember the alligators, elephants and clowns and you'll be fine!

Harmonic Turn Signals

Have you ever wondered how it's possible that a highly skilled improvising soloist can employ all kinds of chord substitutions and seem to telepathically tell the rhythm section what he's about to do? When I was growing up, listening to great players, I'd hear them do this all the time. It seemed like a cool trick, like a magic act. After many years of study, I learned that it's not magic. It's a signal. And a pretty cool and subtle one, at that.

On any given set of chord changes, an advanced soloist can decide to employ a substitute chord. The soloist signals that he's going to play a different chord by starting his phrase with the substitute chord just a bit early. Think of it like a Harmonic Turn Signal.

Let's pretend that you're driving on the highway (as pictured on the previous page), headed to a club for your gig, and your piano player is following you in her car. She doesn't know where the club is located, but she's on the road, right behind you. As long as you're going straight ahead on the main highway, no turn signal is needed.

You were planning to take the G7 chord exit, but at the last minute, you decide that you'd prefer to take the scenic route of Tritone Sub Boulevard. Because the piano player is following you, you put on your turn signal to let her know that you're getting off at a different exit.

In a musical performance, it works the same way. You activate your Harmonic Turn Signal by playing the substitute chord slightly before the measure arrives.

The speed of the song will determine just when you should use the turn signal. If it's a medium tempo, you don't need to signal very early. However, if it's a fast tempo, you might signal farther in advance, so that there's time for the person following to change lanes and easily follow your lead.

The Music examples below demonstrate the use of Harmonic Turn Signals:

Straight ahead on highway I-251 (ii / V / I), no turn signal needed.

Medium tempo, with a turn signal one beat early to indicate the chord substitution.

Fast tempo, with a turn signal two beats early to indicate the chord substitution.

The next time you're listening to a live jazz combo, see if you can notice when the soloist is using his Harmonic Turn Signals to get the rest of the group involved with his chord substitutions.

By the way, you don't need to limit your use of the Harmonic Turn Signals to chord substitutions only. The next time you play the Rodgers & Hart classic, "Have You Met Miss Jones?" try using your Harmonic Turn Signals by playing approximately one beat early on each chord change in the bridge of the song. This will give you a feel for what it's like to anticipate the sound of the new chord change. It creates a really cool harmonic effect, sort of like you're driving a big rig, looking over the tops of all of the cars in front of you, clear to the next key center.

The next time you're playing with a group, imagine that you're the lead car. The other players are following you, listening for your Harmonic Turn Signals to guide them across the country. Time for a road trip!

The Bobber Theory

All professional musicians have a feeling of life and energy in their playing. It's as if their improvised notes are jumping out at you. An aspiring player can have good note choices, great phrasing and a beautiful tone, but one vital piece of the musical puzzle is often missing: a feeling of spontaneous energy and excitement.

This feeling was one of the most elusive elements for me to acquire as a young player because it was so hard to define. I knew how to practice scales and chords, but how was I supposed to practice a feeling of "spontaneous energy"?

After much contemplation, I found a new way to think of this energy, which allowed me to put this abstract concept into more tangible terms. Getting this energy into my playing was a huge turning point for me, and helped make the transition from sounding like a good student to sounding like a pro.

One day while practicing, I had an image in my mind of a man fishing on a lake, using one of those round plastic red and white "bobbers" that moves in the water when a fish takes the bait on the line. Everything is calm, and the man is almost asleep, when suddenly, the bobber moves! A fish has taken the bait.

The bobber is moving, causing waves, and the man starts reeling in the fish. There's a lot of activity in the water. Something in my mind connected this image with musical sounds (maybe it was from watching the movie "Jaws" too much when I was a kid!) and I came up with what I now call "The Bobber Theory."

The core of the theory is that motion is produced when a fish takes the bait at the end of a fishing line. This motion isn't completely steady or predictable, which adds to the excitement generated by the unknown speed and depth of the movements…it might be a small fish biting, or a big fish…you don't know until you reel it in! The movement of the bobber in the water causes waves that tell the man he has a fish on his line. When applied to soloing, those "waves" equate to short, fast breath accents that exaggerate some of the notes being played. (For non-horn players, this would equate to additional pressure on a piano key or on a plucked string.)

There is no hard and fast rule as to what constitutes the "right" amount of extra breath accents, or "jabs of air," as I sometimes call them. It all depends on how much you want to heighten the rhythmic intensity of the line – how big is the fish?

All professional players use this effect, but to hear The Bobber Theory used in a dramatic way, just listen to any Cannonball Adderley recording. He's reeling in the big fish with every solo!

The illustrations on the next two pages show The Bobber Theory in action.

In this picture, notice that the music looks dull and faded. This is because the fish has not yet taken the bait, and the water is still.

In the picture above, notice all of the activity caused by the fish taking the bait. The bobber is moving, the man is reeling in the fish, and there's a lot of excitement. This is indicated in the drawing by the darker, clearer lines of the music notes and staff, and by the new accents over some of the notes.

Apple Chords

Just as there is a range in the flavors and textures of apples, the same is true when it comes to chords. It's common for musicians to describe sounds as "bright" or "dark," but I've taken that concept in a different direction, using synesthesia to identify a chord in terms of taste, using "sweet" or "tart" in place of the usual (visual) "bright" or "dark" labels.

Synesthesia is the mixing of the senses, like seeing the color red in your mind when you hear a concert C, or seeing the color blue when you hear a concert F. In this Apple Chords analogy, I'm equating the character of a chord's sound with the taste of various apples.

This concept came to me very naturally. I was in a practice room with a piano, and I'd just taken a short break from practicing saxophone. I had a Red Delicious apple to eat as a snack. I took one bite of the apple and then played a Cmaj7 chord on the piano. Somehow, my mind started to associate the bright sound of the major seventh chord with the sweet taste of that apple.

This sensation of mixing a sound with a flavor was fascinating to me, and it resonated on a different level than the mathematical, intellectual approach I'd been using to learn my chord spellings. Although chord spellings are extremely important, I found that they were not too helpful when I needed to quickly identify a chord just by hearing it. After this experience with the apple, I started to think about the chords as having distinctly different flavors that could be immediately "tasted" as soon as I heard them.

For example, I noticed that the difference between the sound of a Cmaj7 chord and a C7 chord was that the C7 was not quite as "sweet" sounding as the Cmaj7. Next, I noticed that a Cmi7 chord had a kind of neutral flavor to it. I started to notice a pattern. Each time I added an additional flat to a note in the chord, the flavor of the chord started to sound (taste) more "tart" in my mind. Below, you'll find my original Apple Chord table:

Cmaj7	C7	Cmi7	Cmi7b5	Cdim7
C E G B	C E G Bb	C Eb G Bb	C Eb Gb Bb	C Eb Gb Bbb
Red Delicious (Very Sweet)	Honey Crisp (Sweet)	Rome (Neutral)	Braeburn (Tart)	Granny Smith (Very Tart)

Shortly after I started using this system for my own study, I had an opportunity to try it out on a group of young music students. I was teaching privately at a high school, and the band director told me that he wanted me to give a short presentation on ear training with a visiting group of seventh-grade band students. I had just ten minutes to teach them something, and I decided to try out the Apple Chord concept.

These students had heard of chords before, but they didn't know how to spell them, and they didn't know the different names of the chords. I played a series of chords on the piano and explained that the chords each had a unique sound, and that if you listened carefully, you could tell them apart.

I told the kids that I had a fun, new way to think of the chords, and we started talking about apples. I asked the kids if they could tell the difference between the taste of a Red Delicious apple and a Granny Smith apple. The kids said that it was easy to tell them apart because, as one of them put it, "the red one is sweeter." I explained that just as they could taste the difference between the apples, that there was also a way to taste the difference between chords. I had discovered a way of "tasting" the sounds with our ears.

I started by playing a Cmaj7 chord while saying the words, "Red Delicious." I told the students to think about biting into a Red Delicious apple every time they heard me play the Cmaj7 chord. Then I told them to shout out "Red Delicious" right after I played the chord. I repeated the chord a few times, and then I played a Cdim7 chord. As I played the new chord, I said "Granny Smith," and asked the kids to imagine the tart taste of the Granny Smith apple every time they heard me playing the diminished chord.

Next, I started to alternate between the Cmaj7 and the Cdim7 chords. I asked the kids to shout out the name of the apple that the chord sounded like. After they did this for a while, I started to transpose the chords, playing an Fmaj7 chord and an Fdim7 chord. Then, I started to add more and more chords, always playing either the maj7 chord or the dim7 chord, built from many different roots.

The kids were amazingly accurate. They could really tell these sounds apart, yet they didn't know any chord spellings. Interesting! Next, I told them to say "major seventh chord" when they heard the sound that was like the sweet-tasting Red Delicious apple, and to say "diminished seventh chord" when they heard the sound that reminded them of the tart Granny Smith apple. They did it, and had a lot of fun with it. It really worked!

The band director returned to the room after ten minutes and asked the kids if they had learned anything new. The kids were all smiling and very eager to show off their newly discovered skills. I played the major seventh chords and diminished chords on the piano, and the kids shouted out the correct chord type every time. I explained the system to the director, and he loved it. I told him that I was going to present the system in a future book. That was several years ago, and I'm very pleased to share the system with you.

RED DELICIOUS

Chord	Root	3rd	5th	7th
CMaj7	C	E	G	B
DbMaj7	Db	F	Ab	C
DMaj7	D	F#	A	C#
EbMaj7	Eb	G	Bb	D
EMaj7	E	G#	B	D#
FMaj7	F	A	C	E
F#Maj7	F#	A#	C#	E#
GMaj7	G	B	D	F#
AbMaj7	Ab	C	Eb	G
AMaj7	A	C#	E	G#
BbMaj7	Bb	D	F	A
BMaj7	B	D#	F#	A#

HONEY CRISP

Chord	Root	3rd	5th	7th
C7	C	E	G	Bb
Db7	Db	F	Ab	Cb
D7	D	F#	A	C
Eb7	Eb	G	Bb	Db
E7	E	G#	B	D
F7	F	A	C	Eb
F#7	F#	A#	C#	E
G7	G	B	D	F
Ab7	Ab	C	Eb	Gb
A7	A	C#	E	G
Bb7	Bb	D	F	Ab
B7	B	D#	F#	A

ROME

Chord	Root	3rd	5th	7th
Cmi7	C	Eb	G	Bb
C#mi7	C#	E	G#	B
Dmi7	D	F	A	C
Ebmi7	Eb	Gb	Bb	Db
Emi7	E	G	B	D
Fmi7	F	Ab	C	Eb
F#mi7	F#	A	C#	E
Gmi7	G	Bb	D	F
G#mi7	G#	B	D#	F#
Ami7	A	C	E	G
Bbmi7	Bb	Db	F	Ab
Bmi7	B	D	F#	A

BRAEBURN

Chord	Root	3rd	5th	7th
Cmi7b5	C	Eb	Gb	Bb
C#mi7b5	C#	E	G	B
Dmi7b5	D	F	Ab	C
D#mi7b5	D#	F#	A	C#
Emi7b5	E	G	Bb	D
Fmi7b5	F	Ab	Cb	Eb
F#mi7b5	F#	A	C	E
Gmi7b5	G	Bb	Db	F
G#mi7b5	G#	B	D	F#
Ami7b5	A	C	Eb	G
Bbmi7b5	Bb	Db	Fb	Ab
Bmi7b5	B	D	F	A

GRANNY SMITH

Chord	Root	3rd	5th	7th
C dim7	C	Eb	Gb	Bbb
C# dim7	C#	E	G	Bb
D dim7	D	F	Ab	Cb
D# dim7	D#	F#	A	C
E dim7	E	G	Bb	Db
F dim7	F	Ab	Cb	Ebb
F# dim7	F#	A	C	Eb
G dim7	G	Bb	Db	Fb
G# dim7	G#	B	D	F
A dim7	A	C	Eb	Gb
Bb dim7	Bb	Db	Fb	Abb
B dim7	B	D	F	Ab

The tables above feature the most common spellings for the five "apple chords" in all twelve keys. Note that I have not included all enharmonic spellings. The purpose of this chord table is to provide you with the simplest, most common way to spell the chords. For a complete list of chord spellings, including all enharmonic spellings, visit www.gregfishmanjazzstudios.com.

I recommend that you train yourself the same way that I trained the kids, starting with the two extremes, major seventh and diminished seventh chords. Next, add the minor seventh chord, the dominant chord and finally, the half-diminished seventh chord. It will take some time for your ear to pick up on the differences between all five chord types, but thinking of them as distinct flavors ranging from sweet to tart will give you a huge advantage over someone who simply guesses or tries to think about them in a purely intellectual manner.

Of course, there are more than just these five chord types, but these are the most common chords encountered when playing jazz standards. If you can train yourself to the point where you clearly recognize the unique flavor of each of these chord types, you'll be well prepared to deal with more exotic chords in the future.

If you want to take this analogy to the next level, buy the five apples shown in the drawings. This way, in case you can't conjure up the memory of the taste of the apples in your imagination, you can use the real thing. Bon Appétit!

The Snake

The snake might not be your favorite reptile, but it can clearly demonstrate two different ways of using melodic sequence to make an improvised solo sound more structured and memorable.

Sequence involves the use of repeated melodic, rhythmic, or harmonic patterns. The opening idea, which I call the "Model," is repeated and transposed to fit each new chord. The Model is usually sequenced anywhere from one to three times, at the discretion of the soloist. The Snake gives you two great options for sequencing your ideas.

In the drawing on the next page, called "Snake Around the Rocks," the snake's path represents the way in which the Model is sequenced. In this scenario, the Model idea lasts for the duration of the first chord in the progression. With the appearance of the next chord change, the Model is transposed to fit the new chord, creating a sequence.

The Model in the example on the next page consists of the 9th, Root, 7th, 13th, 5th and 11th of the Cmi7 chord. With the "Snake Around the Rocks," the identical chord tones are repeated in the first and second sequences.

The drawing of "Snake Over the Rocks" on page 73 demonstrates another way to sequence the Model. It's a more complex concept than the "Snake Around the Rocks" approach because it requires that the player have the ability, on the fly, to maintain the melodic shape and direction of the Model while applying different chord tones. It isn't as common as the "Snake Around the Rocks" approach, but it's very effective and exciting to hear.

With the "Snake Over the Rocks" approach, the basic shape of the Model is maintained throughout the phrase, but the chord tones are different for each measure. For example, the first measure includes the 9th, Root, 7th, 13th, 5th, and 11th of the chord; the second measure includes the 11th, 3rd, 9th, Root, 7th and 13th; and the third measure contains the 13th, 5th, 11th, 3rd, 9th and Root.

Snake Around The Rocks

Model   1st Sequence   2nd Sequence

Snake Over The Rocks

Model   1st Sequence   2nd Sequence

"Snake Over the Rocks" sequencing occurs by voice-leading from the last note of the Model to the next closest note in the new chord change. The idea then continues in the same direction as the Model, with an intervallic pattern similar to the Model, but conforming to the new harmonic setting.

The snake "around the rocks" and "over the rocks" are both great for giving your solo a good feeling of melodic development. After you learn how to sequence your Model both ways, it will be your choice as a soloist to decide which path you'd like to take.

Play examples A through C on the next page to get a feel for the difference between sequencing your ideas "around the rocks" vs. "over the rocks." The next time you hear a great solo, listen for the snake, and see if you can tell whether he's going around the rocks or over the rocks.

GREG FISHMAN

THE SNAKE

©2014 Greg Fishman Jazz Studios
All Rights Reserved. Copyright Secured.

Tasting Harmony

For years I tried to find an explanation as to why the seasoned pro can instantly connect with listeners on a deep and intimate level, while the amateur can't hold their attention, no matter how fast or how many notes he may play. The answer: Tasting Harmony.

How can you taste harmony? You can taste it by experiencing the flavor of each note as you play it. Imagine that you're the pro on stage, and instead of your horn, you have a bowl of strawberries on a table in front of you. You take a bite of a strawberry, and as you taste it, the audience also tastes that strawberry. It's as if the signals from your taste buds are going directly to the collective taste buds of the audience. They are *experiencing* the flavor of that strawberry right along with you. I believe that this connection occurs when the same notes you're hearing in your mind are coming out of your horn.

Tasting Harmony – This saxophonist is tasting every note that he plays, and the audience experiences that taste through him.

The drawing on the previous page shows how the professional player connects with the listener. Next, let's look at the aspiring player. Imagine that you're an intermediate-level player working on a song. You've learned the correct chords and their corresponding scales. You may have even memorized some cool licks you took from a recording. However, you're not yet experiencing the flavor of the notes as they're played. The notes are just memorized fingerings or random scale patterns.

I believe that this would be the equivalent of eating the same strawberries we mentioned in the scenario above, but in this case, you've got a cold, and you've have lost your sense of taste. You bite into the strawberry, but it's just texture with no flavor whatsoever. You taste nothing, and the audience tastes nothing. You can try to play fast or high to get the audience excited, but to really reach them on that deep, intimate, emotional level, you must taste the notes as you play them.

Not Tasting Harmony - This saxophonist is not tasting the notes that he plays. As a result, the audience cannot connect with him.

So, how do you go from being the amateur in the example above to being the pro? Many people would just say "practice, practice, practice." However, I believe that's a little simplistic. Of course you'll become a better instrumentalist with lots of practice, but you still may lack that sensation of tasting your notes. That's because you need to do more than simply practice your instrument. You need to immerse yourself in the music and take the time to train your ear to "taste" the sounds you hear all around you, so that every note you play has its own special flavor.

The challenge, especially for horn players, is to hear each melody note as it relates to the chord, and not simply as a series of intervals. Once you start hearing the melody in this way, you'll also start to experience the flavor of the notes as you improvise.

Creating music this way is so much fun and so satisfying, that you'll have a great time whenever you play. When you're having a great time, the audience will be right there with you.

You don't need a ton of technique to achieve Tasting Harmony. It's not about speed. It's about experiencing the flavors of the notes as you play them. The next time you play a solo, take the time to savor the flavor of each and every note. If you can taste it, so can your listeners. They'll be experiencing your music through you and with you, and that's a great thing.

The Music House

When I was seventeen years old, I went to a club in downtown Chicago called The Jazz Showcase to hear Joe Henderson (who later became my teacher). As I sat there and listened to the angular, beautiful lines coming from Joe's horn, I made an interesting observation. Joe looked completely relaxed and calm as he played the most amazing solos. Everything flowed so easily.

I got the image in my mind that maybe Joe was so comfortable because he was in a sort of "Music House." It was a house of sound, which Joe had built through a lifetime of playing. Each room in the house represented one of twelve keys, and the objects in the room represented the various chords and musical ideas Joe would play in each key.

As his playing shifted through many key centers, it was as if Joe was simply walking from room to room in his house, picking up objects (musical themes, variations, etc.), examining them, holding them up to the light, and admiring them before putting them down and going into another room to explore further.

The reason that he could so effortlessly create these incredibly complex solos with such consistency was that he was at home with an entire house full of musical contents.

Like any house, in addition to the furniture, there were personal effects, such as pictures of old friends. Maybe a picture of Charlie Parker was represented musically as Joe quoted one of Bird's melodies in the middle of his solo. Some of Joe's musical structures sounded to me like the sun shining through the deep colors of a stained glass window.

As Joe would go deeper into his solos, I could picture him exploring his house. Maybe he was looking through old picture books and remembering adventures of his youth in far away places. Or maybe he was in his art studio, painting a picture, imagining future adventures.

The Music House

We all need to furnish our musical houses with beautiful melodies, lush harmonies and enchanting rhythms. Make your house like the happy music house in the picture by practicing your instrument in all twelve rooms (keys). Also, be sure to practice in the twelve relative minor keys as well, represented by the small door in each room in the drawing.

Take pride in your house and make sure that it reflects your unique taste and style. People can tell what kind of Music House you keep by the solos you play. Joe's house was a showplace. How's your house looking today?

Close-up view of the Key of C room.

The Kid and the Cupcake

One day, while teaching a lesson, a student asked, "When you're improvising, and you're going to play a scale over a chord, how do you choose your notes?"

His question reminded me of a story from my youth, about a trip to the bakery. The combination of the student's question and my memory of the story inspired me to create this analogy, which I call "The Kid and the Cupcake."

When I was a kid, I loved going to the bakery. One day, as I waited for the clerk to finish up with the customer before me, I studied every cupcake in the display case. Even though all of the cupcakes were supposedly the same, I spotted one cupcake that had a little bit of extra frosting on it. That was the one I wanted!

The clerk asked what I'd like to have, and I asked for a cupcake, pointing to the one I wanted. He grabbed the one next to the one I was pointing at and tried to hand it to me. I shook my head and said, "Sorry. Not *that* one, the one *next* to it, please." He was annoyed that I was being so picky, and he said, "C'mon, kid, they're all the same."

I told him I could see that there was a little more frosting on the one I wanted. He put the rejected cupcake back into the case and handed me the one that I had chosen. I was thrilled! This wasn't just *any* cupcake. It was the *exact* one that I wanted. That made it very personal and special to me.

That's how I choose my notes when improvising. I look for something "special" about the way that each note sounds. I look for that extra little bit of frosting. I'll never settle for the note *next to* the note that I really want. It has to be that *exact* note.

The music examples on the next two pages will take you through my system for practicing the scales on a single-note instrument, such as saxophone, while hearing each note as it blends with the chord. Although I use the diminished scale in these examples, you can use this same system with any scale and chord combination you choose.

I also recommend spending time at the piano, playing the chord in the left hand, while playing each note in the scale, one at a time, in the right hand. Listen carefully to the sound of each note to hear the unique way that it blends with the underlying chord.

In addition, play through the melodies of your favorite songs, and study the notes chosen by the great composers of the standards: George Gershwin, Cole Porter, Duke Ellington, etc. These composers are all masters at choosing beautiful and exciting notes over the underlying chords. I also recommend transcribing the solos of the jazz masters, so that you can study their note choices as well.

By following these suggestions, you'll be well on your way to choosing the special notes — the ones that have that little bit of extra "frosting."

Play through the following examples slowly, paying close attention to the unique flavor of each new scale note added to the chord.

The example at letter "A" shows the original chord. Each additional example, from letters "B" through "F" adds one additional scale note to the original chord. To get a good taste of each new note's flavor, observe all of the fermatas and accents.

©2014 Greg Fishman Jazz Studios
All Rights Reserved. Copyright Secured.

Play through the following example at letter G. Start slowly at first, and then increase the tempo. Pay close attention to the unique flavor of each new scale note as it's added to the chord.

The C7 chord arpeggio played in the first two beats of the measure represents a pianist's left hand playing the basic C7 chord, while the quarter notes on the third beat of each measure represent the sound of a pianist's right hand playing a melody note. I created this approach to help train my ear to hear each note of the scale within the context of the chord on a single-note instrument, such as a saxophone.

©2014 Greg Fishman Jazz Studios
All Rights Reserved. Copyright Secured.

Running With the Pro Dogs

One day while channel surfing, I came across a sport called Dog Agility. It's a sport for dogs in which they run through an obstacle course. At first glance, it might just look like a simple contest to see which dog is the fastest. However, it's not just about speed. Accuracy, timing, skill, and intellect are also involved.

While watching these amazing dogs navigate the obstacles, I noticed many things about the differences between the dogs as they made their way through the course. I noticed that the top-ranked dogs shared key traits, as did the dogs that had trouble completing the course.

The table below compares the differences I observed between the dogs. For the purposes of this analogy, I'm labeling the top dogs as "pro dogs" and the lower ranked dogs as "amateur dogs."

Pro Dog Traits	Amateur Dog Traits
• Having Fun	• Struggling / Frustrated
• Confident	• Tentative
• Focused	• Distracted
• Aware of Surroundings	• Unaware of Surroundings
• In Good Physical Condition	• Out of Shape

The differences in the traits above reminded me of the differences in traits I've observed between professional and amateur musicians.

Pro players have a level of instrumental control that allows them to have fun while playing the music they enjoy in an uninhibited, confident fashion. They're focused on the musical ideas they're developing, and aware of their harmonic and rhythmic surroundings. In addition, they're always in top physical form on the instrument, playing with proper breath support (an essential element for horn players), and with precise technique.

Amateur players struggle because of a lack of instrumental control necessary to focus on the music. It's frustrating to them, because they really want to play well, but they're playing under severe limitations. As a result of not having mastered their chords, they play tentatively, being unaware of their harmonic surroundings. They're unable to keep track of their musical ideas because they're constantly distracted, trying to remember what scale they're supposed to be playing over a chord they can't spell.

In many cases, even if they learned their chords and became aware of their harmonic surroundings, they still wouldn't have the proper instrumental technique to apply all of that great knowledge, because they're out of shape from a technical standpoint. It's almost as if their limitations act like a leash, preventing the dog from leaving the yard.

If we were to simply remove the leash, the dog might run into the street and get hit by a car. That's not a good solution! However, if the dog were trained so that he had the control, skill, knowledge and ability to take care of himself in many different situations, we could safely remove the leash that's holding him back. Then he'd be free to run around the neighborhood, having fun with the pro dogs.

These are the musical obstacles:

• Scales
• Chords
• Intervals
• Repertoire
• Jazz Vocabulary
• Playing in 12 Keys

These are the instrumental obstacles:

• Tone
• Intonation
• Technique
• Articulation
• Dynamics

All musicians, regardless of their instrument, need to work on developing a beautiful tone, good intonation, smooth technique, clear articulation, etc. The practice time necessary to overcome each obstacle will vary, depending on the specific instrument. For example, saxophonists spend a lot of time working on articulation. Brass players are always working on range and endurance. Pianists are working to achieve independent control between their left and right hands. Each instrument presents its own unique challenges to the player.

I believe that aspiring players can work on both the musical and instrumental obstacles at the same time. For example, when working on tone, instead of just playing whole notes, I'll play the melody of a ballad. That way, I'm not only developing my sound, but at the same time, I'm learning a tune, adding to my repertoire.

When working on technique, in addition to reading from an exercise book, I'll often work on a challenging melody, like "Donna Lee" or "Scrapple From the Apple" by ear, in all twelve keys. In addition to improving my technique, I'm also acquiring authentic bebop vocabulary and training my ear at the same time.

While playing my scales, I'll apply many different types of articulation and dynamics, so that I'm not just practicing the scales in an isolated manner. Often times, while practicing scales on the saxophone, I'll play a chord on the piano and hold down the sustain pedal, letting the chord ring out. This way, I can hear how the notes played on the saxophone blend in with the chord on the piano. This allows me to practice my scales while applying them to many different harmonic contexts.

By following the various practice suggestions above, you will improve as both an instrumentalist and as a musician. Even though I was observing a sport on television in which there were winners and losers, with this analogy, you can be the winner every time. As you overcome each obstacle, you'll be one step closer to Running With The Pro Dogs.

About The Author

Saxophonist and flutist Greg Fishman is an accomplished performer, recording artist, author, teacher and clinician. Born in Chicago in 1967, he began playing professionally at age fourteen. Greg graduated from DePaul University in Chicago with a degree in Jazz Performance, and earned a Masters Degree in Jazz Pedagogy from Northwestern University.

He is among the foremost experts on the music of Stan Getz and is the author of three Getz transcription books published by Hal Leonard. His self-published books, *Jazz Saxophone Etudes, Volumes 1 – 3, Jazz Saxophone Duets, Volumes 1 – 3, Jazz Phrasing for Saxophone, Volumes 1 – 3, Jazz Guitar Etudes, Hip Licks for Guitar, Jazz Trumpet Duets, Hip Licks for Trumpet, Tasting Harmony™ and Hip Licks for Saxophone Volumes 1 & 2* are in circulation worldwide and have been endorsed by top educators and jazz performers, including Michael Brecker, Jerry Coker, Bob Sheppard, James Moody and Phil Woods.

Greg is a contributing author of jazz theory articles for *Jazz Improv Magazine, JAZZed, Chicago Jazz Magazine, IAJE Jazz Educators Journal,* and was featured on the cover of *Saxophone Journal,* for whom he also writes. He is the author of the liner notes for the Verve reissue of the Getz recording *The Steamer*.

Greg has toured and performed worldwide with his own group, and with such artists as the Woody Herman Band, Louis Bellson, Slide Hampton, Conte Candoli, Lou Levy, Clark Terry, Jackie and Roy, Don Menza, Ira Sullivan, Judy Roberts, Jeremy Monteiro, Jimmy Heath, Lou Donaldson, Harry Allen, Jeff Hamilton, Eddie Higgins and Benny Golson.

In addition to clubs and concerts in the U.S., Greg has been featured at the *Concord Fujitsu Jazz Festival* in Japan, the *NorthSea Jazz Festival* in the Netherlands, *The Monterey Jazz Festival* in California, and in numerous concerts in Hong Kong, Bangkok, Singapore, China and Israel.

Greg teaches jazz master classes and college workshops nationally and internationally, and is on the faculty of the *Jamey Aebersold Summer Jazz Workshop*. When not on tour, Greg is based in the Chicago area where he performs locally and teaches at *Greg Fishman Jazz Studios*. He also teaches students throughout the United States and around the world via Skype lessons.

Greg Fishman is a *D'Addario Woodwind* artist and plays Rico reeds exclusively.

"...His solos are shrewdly conceived yet delivered with apparent ease and elegance. He develops harmonies that sometimes startle the ear as he forges lines that take unexpected twists and turns..."

— Chicago Tribune

"Greg Fishman dares to explore new musical heights. Every lesson in Greg's books is a must for all musicians. Greg, you've done a beautiful, musical thing again!"

— James Moody

About The Illustrator

Mick Stevens has been drawing cartoons for *The New Yorker* for over 30 years. His work has also appeared in *Barron's, Harvard Business Review, Bark Magazine,* and *The Missouri Review* as well as many other publications, including *The New Yorker* series of themed collections such as *The New Yorker Big Book of Dogs, The New Yorker Big Book of Cats,* and all of the *New Yorker End-of-Year* and *"Best Of"* editions. His cartoons can also be found in *The Rejection Collection (books 1 and 2),* edited by Mathew Diffee, and he's had several books of his own published over the years.

Several years ago, Mick took up the tenor saxophone. At one point, he took a phone lesson, then later a Skype lesson with Greg Fishman. In the process, they had a conversation about Greg's next-planned series of musical instruction books, and Greg invited Mick to do illustrations for them. The result is this book, featuring a number of Greg's teaching analogies, paired with Mick's drawings.

hip licks
for
s a x o p h o n e

by Greg Fishman

Available on the iPad
App Store

hip licks
for
saxophone
by Greg Fishman

Book & Four CD Play-Along Set
for Alto and Tenor

Hip Dominant 7th Licks

hip licks
for
s a x o p h o n e

by Greg Fishman

volume 2
Book & Four CD Play-Along Set
for Alto and Tenor

THE MOST EFFECTIVE WAY TO LEARN THE LANGUAGE OF JAZZ
IS NOW ALSO THE **MOST CONVENIENT**

Greg Fishman Jazz Studios • 824 Custer Ave., Evanston, Il 60202
Ph: 847.334.3634 • greg@gregfishmanjazzstudios.com
youtube.com/gregfishman • facebook.com/gregfishmanjazzstudios

GREG FISHMAN
JAZZ STUDIOS